A Sentimental Garden

HOPE CERNA

DAXSON PUBLISHING

A Sentimental Garden © 2025 by Hope Cerna
ISBN: 9781966337164

FIRST EDITION, 2025

PRINTED IN THE UNITED STATES OF AMERICA

Edited by Christine Michele Estopare
Cover Art & Design by Laura Anne Abbott
Layout Design by Terrence Chouinard

to my mother

Table of Contents

A Sentimental Garden

Biography

They ask me,
who was she?

tell us her story
write us a ballad
dictate a biography
spill poems upon the page

how do you describe someone
already gone?

simple,

she was the little girl,
squatting on the dusty street
waiting out the rain and
her stubborn father's patience
clutching the ill puppy
in her thin arms.

Longing

I think I can sense the future
I felt your end in your silences

pauses that lingered
longer every year.
or maybe the end is just the sort
of future easy to predict.

a sharp memory lingers in the back of my mind.
sharpened by the look in your eyes
that day.
thorns of a wilting rose that dug into my heart,
which is why I remember it so well.

even if that day was just you spontaneously
deciding lunch at a nice restaurant
though you had no money

and I kept quiet because–
I wanted to pretend for a soft afternoon
you were still capable of
taking care of me.
that in innocent confidence
I never saw your struggles.

over one meal,
I saw not my mother
but a young girl longing
for her own mother,
for a simple, clean house
and a bed shared with siblings.
a house lost in a city of memories.
back in the bright days
before you realized your father was
a disappointment,
before he broke your heart.

on dusty roads
you are small enough to still need

your mother's hand

you are not looking at me;
you are looking at something very far away.
fork in hand, I flounder, I grapple, I brave
a question, hoping it's the million-dollar one

"If you could go back to that house, would you?"

the air is choked out of you.
a single tear rolls off your cheek
and into my heart's memory.
you've entrusted me
with the smallest, youngest, weakest
part of yourself.

but you are old enough to know
memories exist in places
no one can reach.
and I am old enough to realize
I can never return you to that place.

So, I stay quiet
and we finish our lunch.

Talking Dogs

Snapdragons are called
perritos,
my mother told me.

but who knows if she's right
she also told me
axolotls grew in rain puddles

kneeling low to the colorful, ruffled flowers
she gripped them with thumb and forefinger
just like how she grabbed
little misbehaving dogs
—but this was tender
adoration in her eyes.

with the proper technique
and pressure
you can make them
bark, talk, live

I don't remember the conversations,
the jokes,
or the laughter.
just dewdrops shaken off
petals

I don't remember a lot.
just the sunlight
and the shape of her
fingers pulling life
from delicate flowers
it's the insignificant things
that last the longest,
that is given the most room
in the house of memory.

Mariscos El Viejito

As the youngest
I lasted the longest
as the carry-on bag.

So I go with you—
everywhere.
thus, I'm lucky enough
to catch the moments
of the girl you once were
of the woman who still dreams.

this restaurant is near-empty
making it easy to ignore
the man with the guitar
singing and walking
here where,
    we all pretend he's not there.

but his song finishes
and you rise and look at him
and I realize you were just waiting
and I'm surprised but not
because I know you and
you are always doing things I could never

you make your request,
he's confused
you forgot the song name,
he doesn't know it
my Spanish is poor
years down the line
it'll make me want to rip my hair out.

especially when I remember
how the guitar strings lift and gain confidence
he's got it. the song lifts
and you with it.
you sing like you were born for it.

a song I don't understand
barely remember
the lonely patrons raise their cameras to you
they can ignore the old man playing
but not you
never you,
you sing to small audiences for no money
but nevertheless, it's an audience,
and you still walk away richer.

My Tia told me a story:

In a country far from home
She had no one,
but a fiance with a large family.
a family that resented her.
why?

she was the second wife
and that was enough.
a young bride with no mother
to guide her,
no father to hold her hand.

then, a big sister came along
and offered comfort no one else gave.

"*Come to the bridal shop,*
choose whatever you want, no—
don't worry; pick whatever you want
Don't worry about it.
I'll get it. Pick something pretty."

when she walked down the aisle
she had someone to hold her hand,
the big sister made sure of it.

when the newlyweds were nearly homeless
big sister made sure they weren't.

from their new tentative love
sprung many, many children

cousins who came to comfort me
when big sister finally left us.

Not Afraid

After getting the news she would die
my mother wanted to get tacos

salt is bad for the liver,
the doctor said,
but his eyes said—
"What does it matter? Let her enjoy the rest of her time."

the doctor never says you have
three months
or six months to live.
it's not like in the movies
no, all he says is—
"You are done."

and I don't wail, scream, or break
like in the movies
at least not externally.
as I take her to get her tacos
I listen to her break the news
to my sister

my sister, who I wish was here instead
of me.

Today

7:00am- Wake up
7:30am- Wake up again
8:00am- Have to pee, check if she's breathing
8:30am- Make your bed, don't go back to bed
9:00am- Hungry, have breakfast. She's having pozole for breakfast for some reason
9:30am- Don't watch TV; you have things to clean
10:00am- Don't forget to check her blood sugar
10:30am- Give her Lactulose
11:00am- Too early for lunch still.
11:30am- Check if she went to the bathroom
12:00pm- Do your taxes
12:30pm- Put in a load of laundry
1:00pm- You didn't do your taxes again
1:30pm- Give her a snack and make sure she doesn't vomit on the couch
2:00pm- Her hands are shaking; check blood sugar again
2:30pm- Make her favorite drink and more lactulose
3:00pm- She naps. She naps for a long time.
3:30pm- Look up from your phone see if she's breathing
4:00pm- Did you feed the dogs? Water the plants?
4:30pm- Make sure she takes her pill, but which one out of her personal pharmacy?
5:00pm- Food
5:30pm- Bloated and tired, but she wants a bath now
6:00pm- Pull her out of the bath
6:30pm- More lactulose. Make sure she goes to the bathroom
7:00pm- Grocery shopping? Now?
7:30pm- Grocery shopping tomorrow
8:00pm- She's going to vomit. Catch it and give her liquids
8:30pm- Don't do online shopping; you don't have the money–is she breathing?
9:00pm- I still have homework to do
9:30pm- She wants tea
10:00pm- Too many text messages I don't want to answer
10:30pm- She's asleep, but for how long?
11:00pm- Sleep
11:30pm- She's awake
12:00am- She's crying
12:30am- Make her tea
1:00am- Still crying

1:30am- Lactulose
2:00am- Still awake, still crying
2:30am- What to do?
3:00am- I don't know
3:30am- What to do?
4:00am- I don't know
4:30am- What to do?
5:00am- Give up call an ambulance
5:30am- They question you
6:00am- Watch them take her
6:30am- Cry
7:00am- Sleep

Stale

My mother's sadness permeated the room
like heavy, wet humidity.
It sank through the walls into the next room.

When things were good,
the sun was shining
and every room felt and smelled
like a Lysol commercial.

But I was used to the not-so-good days.
I nursed on bad days and baby formula.
It didn't taste horrible.
All of it was like soup.

Soup gone room temperature.
Canned soup you can still taste the tin in.
Left to sit long enough, you can start to pick out
the salt grains gathering at the edges of the bowl.

Meant to last long on a shelf, never
meant to last on your dining table

but I spooned it up
bite by bite

silently eating as the light dimmed
in the windows.

Your Son is Crying to Me From the Other Room

A special kind of love
is born
when you wash their hair
      make their food
          change their clothes
          and wipe their ass.
Roles were changed.
I was Mother,
you, my fragile child.
I learned to sleep lightly.
to listen to the tempo of your breathing,
the cries that only came at midnight.

        I bathed you
          learned to wash your hair gently.
but you were too heavy for me to carry—
even as you got thinner and thinner.
Not being able to carry you made me cry
    but it took a special kind of love for me
    to wait until you were gone to cry.

I did not cry; I waited until after.

I think my special kind of love
burned alongside you that day.

your son is crying to me from the other room.
He's in pain.
but I have nothing left to spare.
I can barely look at him some days.

Lift with Your Knees

Let me carry you.
please, let me carry you

all the bones, blood, muscle, and sinew.
I'll carry it all.
until my own bones creak, my blood burns,
but I can't.
it's never as easy as they make it look in the movies.

I leave it to the uncle and cousin,
and all I think of is that this isn't how you wish to be seen.
without wedge shoes or red painted nails.

you're so thin,
I can see your bones.
my hand fits around it.

I feel the weight of your life in every wheezing breath.
I count them.
This is how I watch time pass.

I Used to Work in a Grocery Store

Once my mother picked me up
from work, wearing a chicken onesie I bought her.
She shopped for chorizo in it.

That's it.
That's the story.

On My Way

I drive down ugly, cracked concrete,
familiar fast food joints flashing by.

I see the Ralphs gas station telling me
I'm almost home.
I have my music
that you hate turned up all the way.

The nurses checked you in, and you were doing—
pretty bad.

so I figure I have a couple nights

I'll clean the house, check the plants,
feed the animals,
then I'll lie down, do nothing, scroll my phone
because it's now my own personal holiday.

But it's just a holiday in my head.
I clench my phone,
not seeing the videos
waiting for your call,
waiting to hear your voice
saying—

"I feel better, I want to come home now"

Cold Summer

Waking up that morning, the light of a
New day, a
New year, a
New beginning fell upon me.

It told me the future,
And I already wanted to shrink back into the covers.

Spring would be cold
Summer would be cold
Fall would be blistering
Winter would kill me.

As I draw the comforter tighter around me
already, I can feel it.
The cold air bubbles,
wrapping around my legs,
 gathering at my shoulders.

This morning light is the same as
the light on that morning
my brother knocked
bad news on my door

The morning you left and the cold came to stay.

Waiting

I feel like time is getting all mixed up in my head. Time is divided by when you were there and when you weren't. Did I buy this book when you were alive? Did this happen to me when you were alive, and did you know it? I think I remember these things better when you were around. A sun to tell me the hour by the shadow. The hours crawled by so slowly when I was watching you breathe. Now, it's all racing by too fast. Weren't you just here? How is it September? Weren't we just mourning you as one? What happened to the days I was walking around the house, waiting for you to call me? To tell me to pick you up from the hospital with your sweet accent? I think my heart will always break when I hear an older woman with a little accent. Such good English from trying so hard to learn, but that little accent will always remain. I won't be able to talk to you like that anymore. I want to return to the days when I was waiting for you like a good daughter.
always waiting
waiting.

The Heart

In a place unseen
my heart is splitting open

heartbreak feels like the maw of a shark
devouring me
but the shark is me
and I am the shark

I devour myself

solitude is etching itself into my bones

once again, today, I am reminded of my place in the world
not first, not second, certainly not third place

when no one waits for you, do you matter at all?
with no end in sight, does the journey really matter?
too much of me was taken when she left
half of me returned to dust,
the other half is wandering

Will this ache ever end?
Please, God, tell me it ends?

Blank

there are pages and pages
of blank paper
before me.

all I do is stare
I want to think of
absolutely nothing.

This convenient society makes that easy.

my head is heavy, my body aches, and the words
feel like tar bubbling in my stomach.

I must do something, but my hands
are wrapped around my throat.

Bouquet of Poppies and Gladiolus

I dream of simple things.
I dream of the curve of your cheek as you
turned your head to scoff or laugh
I dream of your animated eyebrows
your large eyes, brown and lively
like a doe, a wild thing.
You were more a lion, though.

You were the dancer at parties
everyone looked at you
You sang when the guitar came out
everyone listened
You followed strays in the streets
until they followed you

In my dreams, you're a moving picture
You belonged on stage,
You wanted to act, graced the live camera twice
a perfect nose and the charisma
to know how to turn it.

There are not enough pages to write about you.
there was too much of you
You left gold dust in your wake and knew it.
there's too much of you
a quiet life as a Mexican immigrant.
a cashier for thirteen years
I wish everyone knew you as you deserved
because I'm crushing under the weight of your memories.
all I'm left with is funeral flowers and the simple fact that—

...my children will never know you.

Smile, The Family is Here

My head is a typhoon
lights flash, and high notes ring
gathering all into a dark center—

a lone black pearl emerges

it sits behind my clenched teeth.

Jacaranda Falls

Soft amethyst-colored blossoms
        litter the dirt ground
A black box covered in lace
        is carried in
Coconut candies, coffee chocolates, and boxes of sayula
        flow from a ribboned basket

Frilled lavender-colored blossoms
        cast a gentle shade over white tables
The burble of pozole can be heard; lift the lid
        and earthy oregano, sharp onion, and the sting of lime flow out.

Scentless lilac-colored blossoms
        decorate the table
Candles of orchid are lit and perfume the air
        the sky darkens and deepens

As a song our blood knows is sang
We inscribe our love and regrets
On silver stars
Our final goodbyes.

We set them free as the jacaranda falls.

Guitars Get Lonely Too

In family gatherings
when the beer gets low
and the grill begins to cool

inevitably, somewhere
from nowhere, out of everywhere
a guitar is brought out

a grandfather's guitar
a father's guitar
a cousin's guitar
a family sound

like moths to a flame, we gather
even if the language
is lost to some
still, we sit, we revere
for music is a language
all understand, even if not all speak it

my mother spoke it very well
she spoke with her soul

my cousin tells me,
"I can't stand it when they bring out the guitar now,
I'm waiting for your mom."

so am I.

Those Who Did Nothing

Venom wells up in my mouth
dripping off the corners of my lips
in a rhythm to resound
the names of those I resented.

My rage is hot and being slowly
tempered into something vile.
the memory of prayer
is all that keeps me merciful

I must be merciful,
for I love them
all too much.

In the lines of my face,
exist the life of my mother
sometimes, I wonder if my
family sees her ghost in
my face just as I see
hers in theirs.

Teach Me How to Pray Again

Too much rage and sadness inside,
hollowing me.
all in the shape of you
but the cavity echoes their names.

I think you believed me to be the strongest.
which is why I was left with all your weight.
and I think I am, or at least was.
because I'm now cracking under the weight
of your absence.
it's heavier than the time I stayed awake
to count your breaths.

you were my pillar, but now I'm in freefall,
and I don't think your children can catch me.
they never caught you.
Mother,
I need you to teach me how to pray again.
my supplications are half-empty without you.

On the Left Side of Grief

There's a strange feeling in my chest.
an unnamed feeling.
what is it?
I can feel it on my heart
like a thin, sticky film.
I can't peel it off.
and I barely feel it, but it's there; it's always there
it doesn't go away even when everything
is peaceful.
slowly reaching into my lungs,
choking off my air.
what is this?
what is this?
what is your name?
why must you exist alongside my quiet?
what are yo—
oh
that's right,
your name is

Guilt

Between us, there is a space

We stretch out hands

embrace each other

call out names loudly,

all in a desperate attempt

to fill the space

someone else left behind.

Like A Bell

There's a ringing in my ear
sometimes a ring
sometimes a hum
sometimes, a soft tick
it's the white noise of my own body
drawing my mind away from reality

but reality always bites harder than the tick in my ear

the moans, the gasps, the whimpers,
the cries, the whine, the sob, the snivel,
the wail, the groan, the sniffle, the mewls,
the weeping.

so much weeping
it leaks in like mist through cracks

the righteousness in me tells me
to go, go comfort, go quiet them

the selfishness in me tells me,
to go into the other room, you've done enough

the resentment in me tells me,
to steel my spine; he deserves it.

the mother in me tells me to go,
he's all you got, and you're all he's got

the child in me tells me
to run to my mother's room and cry

the love in me tells me
to do all these things.

Barbed Pedestal

I've been thinking about freedom again lately
how I haven't thought of it in a while
probably because I'm no longer without it
I had a feeling you were as much as
burden as a pedestal.

I spent so much time lifting you,
I had no strength left for myself
Do I regret it?
no
Do I regret these thoughts?
yes
Do I wonder where I'd be if you were still here?
                    all the time.
maybe I wouldn't so aimless
maybe I'd be nowhere, not having changed a bit.

Sometimes love seems like a winter jacket too heavy
for me to wear.
Sometimes, it feels like barbed wire in the mouth.
Fried Chicken is the Setting of My Grief

A grocery store sets the scene of my grief
I tried to hold back
my tears today
and felt my throat close up.
it felt like choking
like drowning,
like my love grew barbs
I'm drowning myself while making fried chicken.

I hide behind fryers
and ovens filled with rotisserie chickens
thankfully, customers can't see me back here.

Handkerchiefs

Handkerchiefs are everywhere
on the floor
over the armrest,
in the dog's mouth.

you laugh and scoff at the dog
but laugh harder
when you see my parachutes

I laugh and say to you
at least mine aren't scattered
everywhere.

you scoff again
and we laugh again,
always laughing

but yesterday, I threw away all your dainty underwear
because we can't donate that.
the shirts that still smell like you
and the cheap jewelry
I'm still not sure of

the floor is clear of you
and now
all I do
is my own laundry

Grocery Store Parking Lots

It gets bad
when rage and hysteria bloom
in a nighttime parking lot

when the walls of life are closing in
cutting off all exits
running to the parking lot for air.
tearfully telling a father of
the predicament and
only the father
because he has PTSD
printed on his resume
and he recognizes this

the desperate gasp for air.
and this breakdown
happens in the parking lot
because it's messy
it's loud
it's foul
the father being the only witness
but if he's not actually here
then he's not really witnessing it
and that makes this easier

so, the nighttime parking lot
becomes the only solace
on this ghetto block
because it's better here than in there
where customers can see, where coworkers will notice

the last place I want to be when I have a fucking breakdown is work
but this damn society demands I pay to live, so I work to pay more
and so
I let the concrete, the peeling paint,
the moths fluttering at the light pole be
the only witness to my weakness

I break in private because I'm determined to make it in public.

White Hell

If Heaven is a hotel,
then Hell must be a motel.

No one wants to be there
but it's all we can afford.

My Hell is white and square
with a kitchenette
and a shower stall with no glass

I do not leave for three days.

It is very quiet.

Mana from Heaven

The mana from heaven sustains me
lighter than snow, sweeter than honey,
it fills me as I wander the desert

but I do not trudge through the high desert
in search of a promised land
with the curses of pharaohs and soldiers
at my back

I trudge through a deep green forest
bark still wet with morning dew,
moss a carpet deep enough to muffle my steps

the mana from heaven sustains me
but I am not in search of a promised land
I just walk; I walk nowhere
I walk until my knees hurt
because I spend more time in bed
than I should
I outrun not pharaohs but something unseen
something much more dangerous

something within,
in possession of fangs
and poisoned claws
but the path is endless

will this walk ever end?

when you walk to a place of no destination,
is it dyed the color of white absence?
or is it muddied into the black of everything?

I do not know the color of my footsteps
only the ache in them.

I pray for the mana of heaven.

World Pain

I walked through cobblestone streets,
to meet a German girl in a country
neither of us knew.

passing graveyards, grief—
crunches up my heart like a
dirty autumn leaf.

tea and cake between us
I asked the German girl
for twenty-three new names for grief—
for sorrow

"Weltschmerz," was all she said.
a seed for a rose then, it withers

"Weltschmerz."
helium for a balloon then, it deflates

"Weltschmerz."
wind for a sail then, it sinks

"Weltschmerz."
an egg for a robin, then it cracks

"Love is leaving," I cried out.
she nodded sadly; this German girl.
all she said was....

"Weltschmerz."

August 20th

August August August
I just realized it's August
        Your birth month
Even though you never cared for birthdays.
        I wonder if August will
bring me painful things
Like the summer heat that wraps its hands
    around your throat
I wonder if in the years to come
        The shape of August
will always remind me of you.

Planted Westside

By the curve of your cheek
and the line of your back
I could see the silhouette of your heart.

You were a sunflower, always turning
in the direction of the sun.
You seemed to radiate with it,
to drink in the light and to be the light.

I was content to watch,
never checking the mirror for myself.
By the line of my brow
and the curve of my lips,
no need to find out about myself.

You were the sun, and then you weren't.
I drank in your light.

I'm withering.
Nothing blooms here.

Sometimes I wish,
I let the brown center of your heart
devour me.

All I notice now is the smell of wilt.

She Came to Visit

Today, the weight of grief made herself known again,
she sat on my shoulders like a crow
her black baleful beak, whispering
hateful things in my ear.

This morning, grief rolled in like a fog,
making me late for work.
she told me her many names
but I already forgot them all.

Tonight, I can find grief underneath my bed
with a pale face and glassy eyes,
she looked like my mother
she said not a word.

Today, grief strolled in
 planted herself on my vanity,
she brushed her long dark hair and smiled at me,
she had my face.

Tonight, grief finally visits my dreams,
she is absolutely beautiful
and she is the worst of all.

Tiger in a Sentence

Sometimes,
No— often actually
I feel like a tiger pacing back and forth in her cage.
But this is not the interesting kind. Not interesting
at all.
If I were younger, to have such a line applied to me...
I would have felt so cool.
"I" and "tiger" in the same sentence?
Yes, please
But no, not today
Now I know why they pace.
Back and forth in their little cages.
They need to kill the time. They need to burn the youth of themselves before
they realize
they are young still. I am a tiger.
But I have no glory, no strength- I am just pacing.
Habit is incredibly dangerous.
I have forgotten I am even a tiger.
I no longer question the cage; I just pace

Second-Hand Tea

My Depression isn't exactly like I'm Sad
I'm not even sure this is Depression
but–

Right now, my despondency
feels like tea.

A warm cup someone painstakingly
brewed.

and was left to go cold.

Forgotten.

Bad Movies

I remember
watching
bad movies with you.

the hours we spent.

Me
on one side of the room.
Then–You

I still remember
the sensation of splitting
my eyes for you.

Eyeing your breaths,
each change in tempo.
Back then and even now
I believe–
I could've–
done that– forever–.

Picking out bad
movies with you.
watching until
we ran out.
We can laugh at
the bad lines together.

But you were tired.

And truthfully?
 I felt an itch.
a horrible itch
clawing at the
back of my ribs

It was called
longing, that
itch.

longing to go
out, something
new for something
different.

my bones were
too young to
stay in that
room.

I would've stayed with you
I would've stayed with you
forever
I would have.

But I wanted to leave
and you would have let me.

forgive me.

This is the Stage of Reality

I've learned that there are
five stages of grief.

FUCK THAT

Fuck whoever came to that conclusion
It's a thousand stages
They are constantly hitting
Never in order
never in order
Never in order

Order never in

Grief is a perfect word because
it's as heavy
as it sounds.

Donations

I stare at my feet often.
At the very round big toe,
the much smaller toes daintily lined up next to them.
Sometimes I stretch out the arch,
I lift it in the air and make shadow puppets
and pretend I'm someone else.

We had the same shoe size, but your legs were much sexier.
We have nearly the same nose, but yours was smaller,
sometimes, I remember it straighter.
A nose that balanced pride and beauty on a razor-sharp edge.
I wear contacts regularly now but almost regret it
every time I look in the mirror.

How easy it is to go from daughter to mother.

Except your eyes were brighter, a softer, more forgiving brown.
Though in reality, you rarely ever forgave.
I stare at my feet and only my feet because when my eyes travel upward,
to the fleshy leg that gets rounder and rounder–
I remember how little there is of you left.
I have the ass, but you had the legs,
I'm comforted by the fact that maybe you wanted
a part of my beauty as well.
A beauty I can't share, just like I can't share my fuller lips or my bigger eyes.

On our walks, you covered yourself so the neighbors wouldn't see your ruin.
In the end,
I don't think you really wanted to share any of my beauty or my smoother skin.

I do think you wanted a piece of my liver, though.
That's so much easier to give.

If only this country let us see a doctor faster.

Now, all I do is stare at my feet.

Magpie

I gathered up the bits of your existence
like a baby bird trailing after the clumsy farmer
hoarding the seeds of you as much as
my little feathered
fingers can.

a driver's license
a travel luggage tag
a handwritten reminder of your next appointment

I gather these things up to prove you existed,
lived and walked among the ordinary citizens
that still live

I let the junk mail addressed to you pile up for a few days
before I finally toss them.

I left your half-drunk bottle of diet Coke on
the last shelf of the refrigerator door.

when I came back from a cold white country,
it was gone.
.
.
.

I stood staring at the refrigerator door for a little too long

The Fields

My flesh is made of dry-packed clay.
It cracks open at your memory

The sun is burning down,
it reaches pale fingers into my heart and paints it gold.
The light feels like your voice.

I turn with the touch of every breeze; it turns me round
and round, and I–
realize I'm simply looking for your ghost.
But it already lives in my bones.

I wonder if I were to go to that land of corn
and forgiving earth
I'd find your heart there
If I buried myself in that fertile earth,
Will you emerge from it?

Knock Knock

This is a poem I wrote
After therapy.
.
.
.
.
.

But wait, I don't go to therapy.

What am I writing?

I'm knocking on God's door
But he just tells me
I should know already.

Oh,
Oh, I get it.

I'm writing about you again.

Sunnersta

In a cold white room
I let the hours slip through
My hands like mist

In a cold country, I left
windows open, hoping someone
would come to hurt me.

Under a cold gray sky, I walked,
I walked and walked, hoping it
would heal me.

Under a new year, I let the
warm days simmer in me.

Time feels like clear marbles
I'm stringing on a thread.

I'm covered in sunshine now
Even though the sun is gone
            I live.

Swedish Cats

I read somewhere that walking is an important factor
to improve mental health.
beneficial to emotional and
mental health and a good way to get
daily exercise every day.

so when I banish myself to the moss and trees
of Sweden, I practice walking,
over wood bridges
past creeks
sinking into rainfresh moss
fairytale trees blocking out
the gray sky.

I drag myself outside
fighting against the water pressure of my grief
with no stress or obligations to distract me
my sorrow walks beside me,
the moss muffling its steps
hiding in the shadows of the
two pm sunset.
I walk past it,
I try to outrun it
but I hurt my knee on a slope
and I realize how weak I've become
maybe not getting out of bed until 4pm
isn't good.

so I walk,
    past the sleepless nights,
    the dull afternoons
    past the neighbors I can't greet
I walk,
  past dreams of another time
  past regretful conversations
  past that one doctor's visit

I walk deeper into the woods
hoping to bury memories

of sobbing
of paramedics questioning me
of helplessness

I walk into moss and snow
and try not to get lost
    try to forget
    try to focus on my legs, my blood
    try not to imagine disappearing
    try not to imagine how long it'll take for anyone
    to notice
    try to remember the way home
 try to remember what makes a home a home–

In these gentle woods
and I met a cat.
I meet many, Swedish cats are
very friendly.
I pet them,
and they become my companions.
I follow one into the woods
and I remember what it was like
to believe in witches and fairytales
and magic hidden in every corner.

I walk out of these woods
and think of something else.

The Heart II

In a place unseen
my heart is splitting open

heartbreak is like the crushed paper
of a chrysalis

there is pain and darkness
and then there is
light, air, color

the nectar of life pours down my throat
by a loving hand
nectar sweet and cool
nectar hot and tart

once again, I'm reminded of my place in the world
not one, not two, not three,
but twenty letters arrive at my doorstep

memories greet me at the door
and I wave my gratitude to them
when the journey ends, the next one must begin
a piece of me returned to dust
the rest of me wonders

when will love return?
Please, God, when will it all begin anew?

Belonging

I put a hand to a tree one day
and paid attention to its bark

 the rough, damp skin of the tree
called out to me

I felt a ghost pass by
—my younger self
who did this every day once.

this ghost whispered to me
"when was the last time you stood underneath the sky?"

another ghost came
and put her hands over mine

they were my mother's,
who belonged in the garden.

Haunted

The woodgrains
the ceiling panels,
grooves and hollows
of this house are as familiar as
my body

this house is my body
I traverse it in dark confidence
new cracks I sense
the same as when I lose
a single strand of hair

this house has lost something else
something bigger
lighter, heavier
than the cracked window panes,
or peeling paint.

I no longer walk in dark confidence
in this house.
I stumble, trip in the hollows
left behind by someone else
crash into walls suddenly,
overgrown, now,
that there is no one
to warm that wall
with their shadow.

making tea for myself
and only myself
a question arises

will I ever grow accustomed
to the too-wide rooms?
the too many coffee mugs?
the familiar stain on the bathroom wall?
somedays I feel too small for myself
I certainly am too small
to ever grow into this house

I will never fill it.

but I can fill these shoes,
she left behind
not metaphorically–

literal shoes
same size, off-brand uggs, brown,
fur-lined up to the knees

I wear them for the first time
in a house
with an unfamiliar ceiling,
stainless smooth white paint.
the lock on the door making a different sound.

slipping into those familiar shoes
I feel a vague outline
an imprint of a thousand steps
made by someone else

a shape that will never be recreated
will never walk this earth again

I walk in a rain-slicked city in them
share and spill tea with friends on them
crush rings of mushrooms in them
miss my train in them

I walk, run, and shiver in them
hoping they'll keep me close to that person
even as I forget they're on my feet

when I return to my small home,
finally turn the key the right way
and slip off these worn boots
I call my own

I realize the imprint is gone

stamped out by a thousand steps
of my own
and that is okay.

A Bounce House

At my mother's funeral
they ordered a bounce house

Why? because this is a
goddamn party, that's why.

the children will laugh
and play.
we'll sing, we'll laugh
we'll dance with feet
lighter than our hearts

she knew we'd meet again
we all will
so we'll dance, we'll play
the children will laugh
we'll throw our heads back
with the strength of our celebration
She would have been the loudest

no matter where I go,
where I end up
in the room, whoever laughs the loudest
I see my mother there.

Eggs

my head feels like scrambled eggs

our minds and hearts can be blown to smithereens,
yet our body still has the sense to tell you
to get tissues, drink water, put on chapstick

loneliness is a hell I've long grown used to
but damn me if I didn't choke on the ashes
every now and then

hell isn't the screaming place of pitch-black and
flaming reds and oranges
it's quiet, white, in all neutral colors
of sand and snow

My mother once recounted an old conversation
*"Depression is like having a mind that tells you to die
in a body that desperately wants to live"*

Everyone lives in their own little kinds of misery
but I drink my tea
and pet the cat
because we must go on
I must go on
there is something at the end of all this
I promise.

Silent Awe

I touched a moss-covered tree
and felt poetry at my fingertips

poetry is just awe–inspired

I saw sunlight being filtered through
hundreds of trees
the sun painted itself
on plains of snow
lights collided in the sky and
danced in white and green
gleaming snowflakes,
tins of tea,
slugs and caterpillars,
rain and stones.

I lived beside these things in silence
and thought,

oh, so this is it
this is what all those writers and singers
were talking about

I get it now.

forgetting myself is not too bad.

To-Do List

Every night, I make a new To-do list
Every morning, I fail that list

I cross out the calendar
in green,
for good days.
in red,
for the bad ones.

This is a game
of cat and mouse.

I cry when my teeth sink
into myself
I hiss when I'm not fast
enough to escape my claws

this contradiction
is self-love

I examine myself
because I refuse to fail myself

I will escape the beast
I will sink fangs
into tender flesh

                    and eat well...

In the Hall of God

My mother's absence is a red-raw sore
that flares across muscles and windpipes
every time I dare to speak

My mother's voice is how I
learned to spell Jehovah's name
Isn't it proper that the one who birthed me
taught me who created me?

throat raw with prayer
to plead is to exhaust
you forget the rules of life

lying down in small, quiet rooms
everyone can hear me desperately try
to forget myself
they hear me but remain silent
for the sake of decency and humanity

Saying, "Hello, Good Morning," is so damn hard.

To forget all the parts of myself
to be the fallen ice cube kicked under the fridge
let me slowly melt,
maybe someone will remember me before they forget me

to accept this is to deny everything
I've shattered in so many pieces
I forgot how big love made me.

I don't know how I'll die
but my life is singing the names
of those who reached for my hand first
I don't number my days
with time
but with tea
I brew for others

Sweet for her
Green for him
Mint for my mother
Black for remembrance
Chrysanthemum for deliverance

I want to be the fragrance
of black apricot tea
in a cracked and shoddy cup.

I can not speak but
the incense of my soul
will someday reach
the one who taught me god's name

Couplets for What?
Previously published in The ClayJar Review

Let me hide in the house,
witness my grief

I'm not hungry,
stomach bloated to bursting

I have a very straight nose,
it's an altar I place my love on

remember to turn over the garden,
I can't stop reminiscing

life is an airport gate,
hold my hand, I can't remember the way home

conversations are easy to start,
I've pulled teeth practicing this

everything is a long-winding mountain road;
where's the exit? everything must end

I made a childish wish,
I wish things lasted forever

libraries are just a thousand possible futures,
every choice is a courageous act

deserts are so quiet,
there's no such thing as desolation

to be an old lady hosting tea parties for children,
trust in a porcelain heart

something in me has aged,
what's the difference between aging and withering?

raindrops on roses,
purple blossoms on ashes

silver regrets, golden hopes
I just want to imagine a future

ocean vuong's beauty, mary oliver's peace
what will I be filled with?

apple-sweet days, lemon-lonely nights
breathe, blink, breathe, blink,

God promised me peace,
I'm almost there

Dust

I lay down on dark earth,
cushioned by moss.

I lay down in the open land,
shadows of Joshua trees patterning my skin.

I lay down in a white-walled studio,
the cement cold and hard.

I lay down in the garden,
seeds of guaje and guava sticking to my hair.

I lay down in my childhood bedroom,
and count my heartbeats.

Close to the ground, to the earth
as much as possible.

I let my skin think and ponder the world

all the dust we are
all that is
dust to dust, ashes to ashes.

whether it be the dust of the ground
the dust in my hair,
or the dust in a black box
sitting on a shelf.

I lay on the ground and remind myself–
I am dust.
and from dust springs life.

Weightless

I often have dreams of a blinding sun
and the rise of dust clouds

I pass through the wind in those dreams.

After I achieve something
I'm left wondering what are the parts of myself.

I wonder these things in a very small room
with very old walls.

I've skipped over seas and mountains
breathing in sights I can't write about.

> yet I carry that small room with
> me everywhere.

I once slept in the room of my mother's mother.
As she lay back she told me she knew she'd sleep well.

For me, all I think of is the stains
on the mattress.

I think the lines on a ceiling can tell us all about life.
I find my mother's face in them.

Today, I picked up a piano in the rain,
there's a poem in that, I think.

I hope to play a song that sounds
like rain one day.
I would disappear in it.

Dandelion Memories

Dandelion delicate conversation
act as a palette knife on the clay
of one's mind.

sorrow turns us into watery slip
use it right and it can be binding
continuously, persistently it cuts away
to what was always there.

"She had so many clothes, but only ever wore blouses and tiny shorts huh?"

"My tia always wore wedges huh? I always imagine her in them"

"In mom's pictures she always has red nail polish"

My mother once took off her wedges to
chase a rooster my uncle promised her,
–if she could catch it.

My cousin was startled to see
wild hair bobbing outside
the window

but he knew it was her; they all knew it was her.

when we all gathered under a blossoming tree
all our memories matched.

I shall write of dandelion memories forever.

A Sentimental Garden

I don't know how survival works
I thought I did.

I can barely spell *living*
with my tongue, much less
speak of what *thriving* is

My passion tucked
into ninety-degree angles of drywall
fetal position, eyes closed.

But today...

today, I accidentally wander
into the garden.

Nearly blasted myself with the icy hose-water
leaves cracking underneath my feet
drier than my worn-out eyes
I enter the garden
with something other than my sorrow.

I pass flowerless shrubs
and remember past summers
of dolls made with
flower petal dresses and pollen balls

puppeteering snapdragons
to tell all the best jokes

a carpet of pink guava,
seeds clinging to baby teeth

the nopales I barely know how to cut
this odd leafy bush I have no name for

but I imagined cities built
on every cobwebbed leaf

but this is a summer of wither,
the wisteria and
pomegranates are dying.

And yet,
hiding among the brown fire hazard stems
a brave little sprout sits
reaching for the sun
delicate and proudly green
tiny.
already I read
futures written
on its fragile green veins.

Last year,
the pomegranates were sour as regret
but there they were,
not sour enough to deter
the hungry birds

I can't remember the last time I was here

The only difference between dirt and soil
is one is fed with loving hands

My hands are awkward and weak
but they've been loved well
love is abundant spring water
spilling out of cupped hands
an overflow that sprinkles
to the ground.
feeding something other than myself
I understand what that one part
in the bible was trying to say.

As I pour my love onto the thirsty ones,
I forget what I was suffering for
I dig, water, scoop, and prune.
Alongside this garden
I will slowly thrive.

The Inheritance of Love

Did you know after a while
all love appears the same?
I swear, once you love someone
long enough, you'll get it.

A beloved face,
over and over, that face determines
when the day begins
more than the rising sun or
the crow of the rooster.

The lines,
the tears,
the gray,
the sickness,
so much abuse that face suffers.

But still, that face never changes for me

I'd know you as a baby,
I'd know you if you were withered roots
I'd know you in my daughter's face.

I love you so much,
I don't see your face anymore.

It never changes.
It's always the same.
not even liver failure touches it.
What a miracle.

It never changes
It's always the same.
A miracle no one talks about.

I pour love into an empty space,
but one day
I'll have someone
who will inherit

your face.

Just as I inherited the love
you once gave
to a face buried in an old country.

Kinstugi

When she died
I thought I ran out of things
to pray for

now, I pray for
myself
because love always
finds a way through the cracks

I'm broken pottery
placed on the altar of god
by a sentimental child

and god counts
all my gold veins.

365 Stars

Love is inscribed
on 365 paper stars

Love goes beyond gold or diamonds
it's brilliance hidden
in the folds of ink and paper

With patience
I inscribe my love
onto stars
neatly fold them
for a proper deliverance

365 to help get through the days
when the ache sets in from
old bones
and an older heart

I whisper my love onto grass paper
and kiss the stamps
I paint love
on the biggest canvas found

For all my ambitions
none feel purer than this

Please, God, let me be well
be healthy
be wise

let me live long enough to say—
I love you again and again
and again.

In this late afternoon

I invite silence in
and reject clamor;

in my garden, parasites grow
choking the peaches,
pomegranates
and dark mulberries.
dutifully, I pull every weedling

I kneel to the earth
with patient fingers and
forgiving spade.

I pull selfish roots
from deep black soil,
sweep it all away

More will sprout
but I am here now—
finally returned—on my humble knees
freeing the garden

The earth is quiet—
it only whispers
that I linger a little longer.

Lessons

She tells me to rub lemon on my wounds
to rub mango skins on mosquito bites
and to wrap burning mint in cotton for earaches.

She tells me how to walk,
walk like a rooster, a very proud one,
head up, tail up, and chest out.
She tells me how to walk in heels.
She loves to demonstrate.

She tells me the right way to
string a mayate.
Together, we put flying glittering gems on a leash.
The best party trick.

She tells me how to get back at men.
To break their guitars and smear mayonnaise on their clothes.
Though I've yet to have that opportunity,
I can only hope I have her nerve when it happens.

She tells me how to cook and how to dance.
though, unfortunately, I'm a poor student.
Who needs to learn to cook rice when I can make cupcakes?
Surely, we can live off that every day, right?

And dancing is a subject I will not touch.

She tells me she loves me.
She tells me to water her flowers and pray
to Jehovah.

I tell her I love you in these ways.

I walk like a rooster
I rub lemon on my wounds and lick them
I hand mayates on strings to my niece and nephew
I remember men have nothing on me.
I cook rice, pozole, albondigas, and cookies because we still need something

sweet.

and I wait for the flowers to bloom.

Real

Everyone tells me she'd
be so proud of everything
I'm doing right now.

But honestly, I can't imagine that.
I can't imagine her saying
"I'm so proud of you"
that woman was so fucking nonchalant.
I'd tell her what I'd be doing
and she'd shrug and go back to her music
and say
"Of course you are."

Nail Polish

"Seize the minute"
is the name of the nail polish
I paint on your nails a couple times
and the last time.

You flutter your nails at my Tia,
even when you needed help walking,
you still held tight to glamor.

my sister and I find glamor
in all your buried pictures
red in that beauty competition
red when you fix my sister's dress
red when you kiss my father
red in that last hospital visit.

I paint my nails when I travel
when I'm alone
when I'm afraid of everything,
but confident my mother's color can't be
torn from me
but it can happen
anything can be stolen.

I'll still smile and flutter my nails
my blood is, after all, red.

Dappled Sunlight

Exhaustive nights and sorrow
and years of learning to do taxes
was enough to kill dreams of whimsy

Dreams of color and sensation
that shocked more than reality
have all left me like air bubbles
rising from the ocean floor

Now, the only bubbles I see
are the ones rising
from the alka seltzer tablet

The clock in and clock out of society
is meant to put a roof over my head
But the Timekeeper is Kronos, asking
for a bit of my soul—

Yet, in my life of repetition
a spark ignites in the bonfire of my mind
The sunlight is golden
the garden leaves a verdant green
the grit of concrete steps under my feet
and the touch of something small and alive
in my palms

In a scenery new and familiar
I pull back branches and discover...
chicks, rabbit kits,
mice pups in my hands
kittens at my ankles
I carry them like jewels
I pull them from the bushes
like berries
this bedewed cradle of dreams
serves as a reminder,
                    —a lesson.
Dream,
dream, and remember.

Wake up,
wake up, and remember
you are alive.
you are as alive as you wish to be.

nothing lasts, yet everything is growing
and being born
life begs to be held gently,
so be gentle, be kind
we only fear the end because
we are grateful to life.

so let the warmth of others seep
into the bone where memory lives.
no matter how short it may be.

Noon

At noon
I got up from bed and didn't
turn on the drowning music

Instead,
I opened all the curtains and windows
and even the kitchen door,
did some chores.

it was so quiet as I did the dishes
for once, it wasn't painful.

outside, the sounds of life rang
singing birds
wind sighing through the trees
the crunch of dry weeds and sand,
underneath my cat's foot.

sound

not noise

for once, I could hear myself think
and it didn't torment me.

The Postman Must Think I'm Popular

Not only do I have
cousins, and faceless
tia's crowding
my old door

But monogrammed letters
with greetings
and scriptures
stacked on slim borders

Once, my grief was a pendulum
hanging over my neck
whispering through each turn,
the same thing over and over again–

"Your sorrow will go unanswered."
"Your sorrow will go unanswered."

as I'm stabbed into the pit

"Your sorrow will be swept under the rug."

But we were not forgotten,
we,
the ghosts in the room
always hovering at the edge
fading faster than the eye can catch

yet, comfort
was tentatively offered
by the gentle, meek ones,

thank you.

A Dark Beauty
For Layla

a border of a wood fence or a bedroom wall
is how we spoke
it separated us, but we talked often
more than people do today with their screens

first, with the pounding of fists
a morse code turned competition
harder each time until the mothers came to yell at us
then we'd run to the fence
to yell, scream, and holler
names in the courageous way only
children have.

then that fence
became the awkward drive-thru
as our mothers
forced us
to deliver
food
they made.
you, in your threelayers
of drug-store makeup
me, in my red tartan skirt
matched with striped thigh highs.

and then there was the music
only the music
thumping between the walls
a morse code of existence,
with no meaning
informing us of each other's presence
but not of our hearts.
those were the most silent
days of all

Then, tears that have the notes of heartbreak
and the gurgle of an infant can be heard
nothing echoes back

it is my regret.

then, the echoes of the dying began
tears that taste of fear, uncertainty,
and hospital aloe wipes.

called strong and brave, but
that smell still turns my stomach

a dark beauty
that will never know her own beauty
held me at the cracks
with small hands as familiar as my own.
palm lines that told the story of our childhood
our screaming matches, the poisoned words,
the first secret, trust that flowed freely as a
storm-swollen river.

we were the witnesses of our mother's regrets,
examined the scars, and mapped out our
future with it. you swore to be different,
I swore to never change.

we slaved over paychecks or final semester grades.
we forgot the language of children
our names stopped requiring a full lung
but when the ambulance came
the first, the second, and the third time
you didn't scream.

it was a whisper in the dark
that sewed up tight
the years of silence
between us.

and the banging on the bedroom wall began again,
a music of cousins.

Warrior
For Andrea

the singing hum
of a flying arrow
is as familiar as
the gentle keys
of a worn piano

eyes are not needed
to know it's there
the arrow in the sky
chords of the piano

just as the earth waits
for the plunging arrow
you wait for my grief

just as the song begins its overture
you sort through the shattered pieces
of myself

know them
recognize them
hand them back to me
identify them better than I do
possessing a warrior's courage.

the courage to stand at the edge of warfare
and not flinch, not turn from the bloodshed

you do not flinch at the grim thing
I've become.

you wait,

patience a sword you wield well,

thank you.

Honey and Ashes
For Melissa

Sometimes, you have no choice but to ask for help
pride flies out the window

when you are hanging on the edge of a cliff
stuck at the bottom of a flooding well
broken at the bottom of a staircase

broken, fearful, bleeding
calling out for help
praying, praying, praying
someone to hear,
hear and help

a black box and a small plastic tube
is the edge of my cliff
why do humans feel the need to
make everything a monument?
from dust we came, to dust we return
simple,
acceptable,
except it's not.

so I type out H.O.N.E.Y. on my phone
and beg for relief
beg for it
like a cup of warm milk
like the pat of butter on warm toast
like a sore throat
beg for honey to soothe
this ache
this herculean labor

with gentle hands, take
the ashes of my love and grief
and help me remember it

because everything is worth remembering
just as I remember this sweet favor

.

.

.

thank you

The Gleaning
For Ruth

There are loud women
brash women
weak women
proud women

women like the breaking of glass
and the crumple of aluminum cans

then there's you
gifted with the name of friend,
compassion, grace.

if God were to write a song
of you
it'd be like,
the soft sigh of opening buds
unfurling leaves
the rustle of satin and cotton.
a laughter
that is gentle and true.

a friend who makes kindness
an art
beautiful and inspiring enough
to make one attempt art
without fearing the failure

You put me under the sun again.

A Promise

I never realized the histories of your life
were just prophecies of my future

I wear your face, and some days I wonder
if I'll wear your heart as well.

I look at my country
and wonder if I'll flee from it like you did.
only to spend the next forty years missing it.

Red's our color
and tender bruises are harder to pick out on
our red, red hearts.

I felt too much as a child
and I taught myself to stop when the leers and jeers
from those I admired became too much.

You felt too much and never stopped
Maybe that's why I felt diminished as an adult
at thirty, the pain of seventeen came and haunted you
at sixty, the pain of twenty-three came and choked you
at forty-eight, your sisters came to remind you
of the pain of yesterday and of tomorrow

you went and raged in a garden too small to contain it
but you still loved with as much love to make a garden grow
My thumbs may not be green, but
my fingertips are black with the ink of honoring you

where you failed, I will flourish
where I failed, I will remember your garden.

This is a promise.

Naming an Ordinary Afternoon

The afternoon light
streams in beautifully
through my kitchen door

I remembered to sharpen this knife
before slicing through the carrots,
onions, and peppers
It works better than before,
everything works better now.

The burble of my soup
and the hiss of my roasting ham
is a music sweeter than the kind
that falls on ears
this is music that falls on the heart

No loud rock, no obnoxious pop, no
wailing heartbroken diva to assault my ears
and flow into a tired brain–numbing it.
A flood to drown out everything.

But today, with the all the doors wide
open, I can hear the clucking of my
roosters.
That, too, is music.

I polish off this day with
rosemary and thyme.
This time, the herbs won't be
forgotten and left to wilt,
in the fridge.

No, I remember now
how to cook and clean
I finally figured out how to dice an onion
finally figuring out that cleaning is
not for anyone's benefit
but my own.
I remember that I, myself,

am not a chore
put on the bottom
of the cleaning list

kittens and chickens
crowd my kitchen door
curious of me now
that this house is open
and awake again

as I feed them
and myself
I realize that this simple
act of living is also music

I am music,
finally tuned right.

Farewell

this is the longest goodbye
as I write
as I cook and clean
as I drive down old streets
as I handle bright blooms
as I breathe goodbye to you

an act of devotion I will
continue all my days
until I am gray and withered

the grand and small acts of life
are colored by my goodbye
a gentle wave of the heart
as I try to be kind to myself
because more often than not
pain is pointless

my life will be illustrious
an envy of storytime adventures
an inspiration to the quiet
even when age blinds me
and aches bind me
I will speak
speak of love
of pain
of regret
of my life and yours

stories to remember
and to learn

I will breathe goodbye
until the next breath
is hello

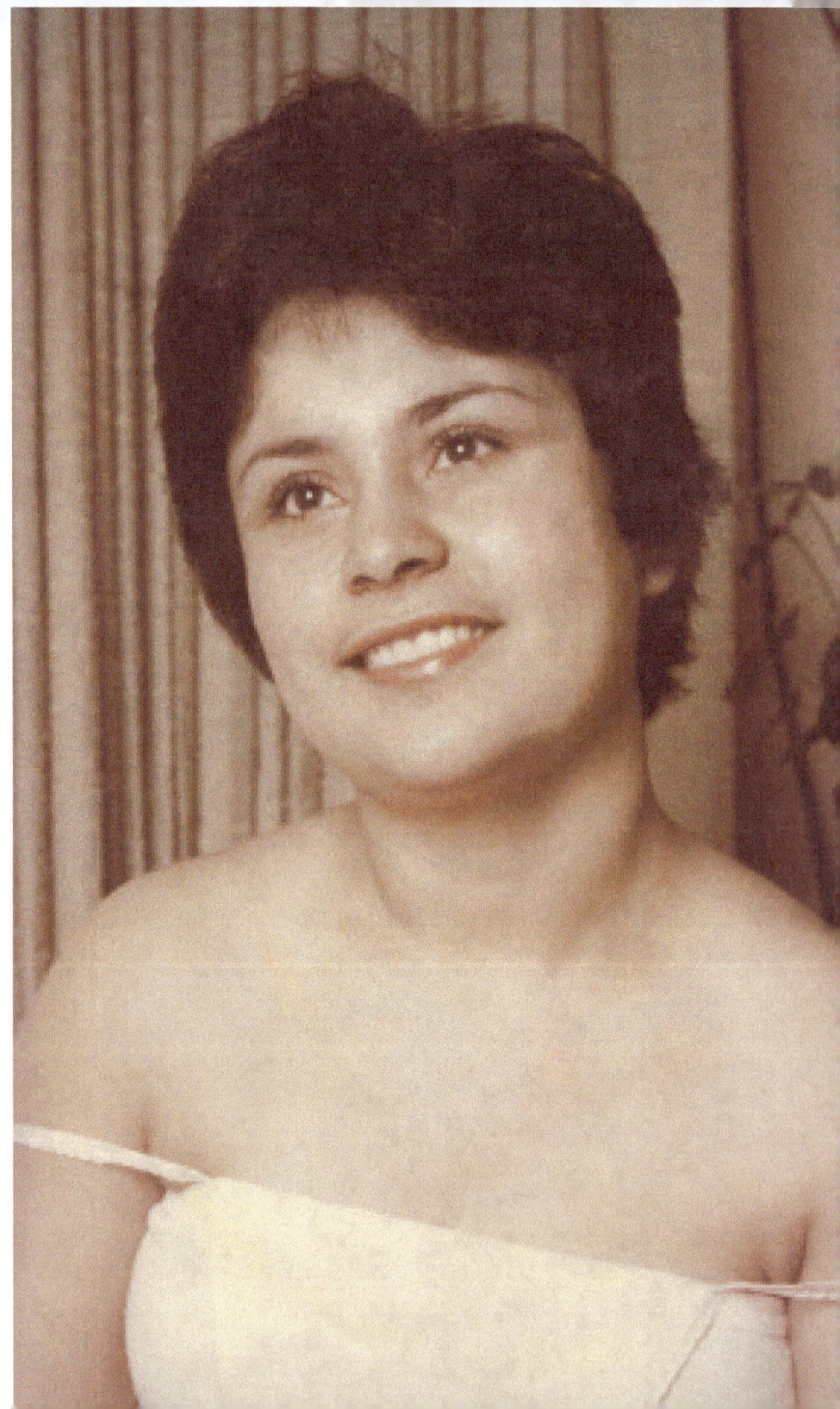

Acknowledgments

To all the readers who've made it this far, thank you. Writing in all its forms is not easy. Especially when writing about the deepest, most vulnerable parts of yourself that you don't even want to look at, much less show to anyone else. But still, you picked this book, read and hopefully digested it peacefully. Thank you.

I thank all the English teachers in my life. If not for my seventh grade English teacher, Mrs. Spencer; I probably never would have dared to dream myself a writer. But she gave me the dream, and I've held steadfast to it all these years. This small dream has been my compass in life. And I'm glad that this compass led me to Hiram Sims and his program, the Community Literature Initiative, and to Karo Ska, my Thursday night teacher. From their love of poetry and expertise, I've experienced what it means to turn a dream into reality.

And my father, who encouraged these dreams all my life. Who never doubted me, never questioned me but jumped on my ridiculous dream wagon every single time with more enthusiasm than myself.

To all the friends and family who were there at my strongest and, most importantly, at my weakest.

And most of all, thanks to my mother. The strongest and most beautiful person I ever knew. Who not only made me but made me who I am. Because of her, I believe in God, myself, and the abundant goodness of the world. I hope this book brings some goodness into the world.

Hope Cerna is a San Fernando Valley native. An alumni of Cal State Northridge and the poetry program Community Literature Initiative. Writing since childhood she hopes to create a space for readers to breathe, relax and dream in her writing. Her work has been published in anthologies Poems in Praise of Libraries edited by Hiram Charles Sims, Artistry of Southern California: Art Poetry edited by Don Campbell and Haiku Crush 2024 Best Haikus anthology. Other pieces can be found in online literary magazines like The Clayjar Review. When she is not writing she can be found rolling dough and frosting cakes.

Publisher's Note

Daxson publishing was created to help marginalized artists and their allies publish their work, so the world can hear their voice. The vision for this publishing house is to help people get their work out there, and not have them struggle finding their way through the publishing process. Everyone's voice deserves to be heard, and we are here to help. If you are interested in submitting a manuscript, email daxsonpublishing@gmail.com.

Support our cause! Buy our books at daxsonpublishing.com.

* 9 7 8 1 9 6 6 3 3 7 1 6 4 *